Phonics

Written By:

Kim Mitzo Thompson

Karen Mitzo Hilderbrand

Artist:
Mark Paskiet
Goran Kozjak

Cover Design:
Steve Ruttner

Visit Our Web Site
http://www.twinsisters.com

Twin 405 - **Phonics** - (Tape/Book Set) - ISBN# 1-882331-23-0

Copyright © 1996 Kim Mitzo Thompson and Karen Mitzo Hilderbrand, Twin Sisters Productions. All rights reserved. No part of this publication may be reproduced, stored in a retrieval system, or transmitted in any form electronic, mechanical, photocopying, recording, or otherwise, without written permission of the copyright owners. Permission is hereby granted, with the purchase of one copy of **Phonics**, to reproduce the worksheets for use in the classroom.

Twin Sisters Productions - 1340 Home Avenue Suite D Akron, OH 44310

Table Of Contents

ACTIVITIES: SHORT VOWEL SOUNDS
Short Vowel Aa..3
Short Vowel Ee..4
Short Vowel Ii...5
Short Vowel Oo..6
Short Vowel Uu..7
Short Vowel Review...8

ACTIVITIES: LONG VOWELS and Y
Long Vowels a,i,o,u, silent e........................9
Long Vowels a,i,o,u, silent e......................10
Long Vowels a,i,o,u, silent e......................11
Long Vowel Sounds ai, ea, ee, oa, ue..............12
Long Vowel Sounds ee, oa..............................13
Long Vowel Sounds ea, ai..............................14
Y As A Vowel..15

LYRICS: "Rhythm, Rhyme and Read" - Phonics
Lyrics: Consonants.....................................16-19
Lyrics: Vowels..20-23
Answer Key...24

© 1996 Twin Sisters Productions — Twin 405 - PHONICS

Short Vowel "a"

Short "a" sounds like the "a" in apple.

Add the correct letters to the words below. Say each word.

__ a __

__ a __ __

__ a __

l __ m p

__ a __

b __ g

Short Vowel "e"

Short "e" sounds like the "e" in egg.

Add the correct letters to the words below.
Say each word.

_ e _

_ e _ _

_ e _

_ e _

n _ s t

_ e _

Short Vowel "i"

Short "i" sounds like the "i" in pig.

Add the correct letters to the words below. Say each word.

__ i __

__ i __

__ i __

f __ s h

__ i __

g __ f t

© 1996 Twin Sisters Productions   5   Twin 405 - PHONICS

Short Vowel "o"

Short "o" sounds like the "o" in fox.

Add the correct letters to the words below.
Say each word.

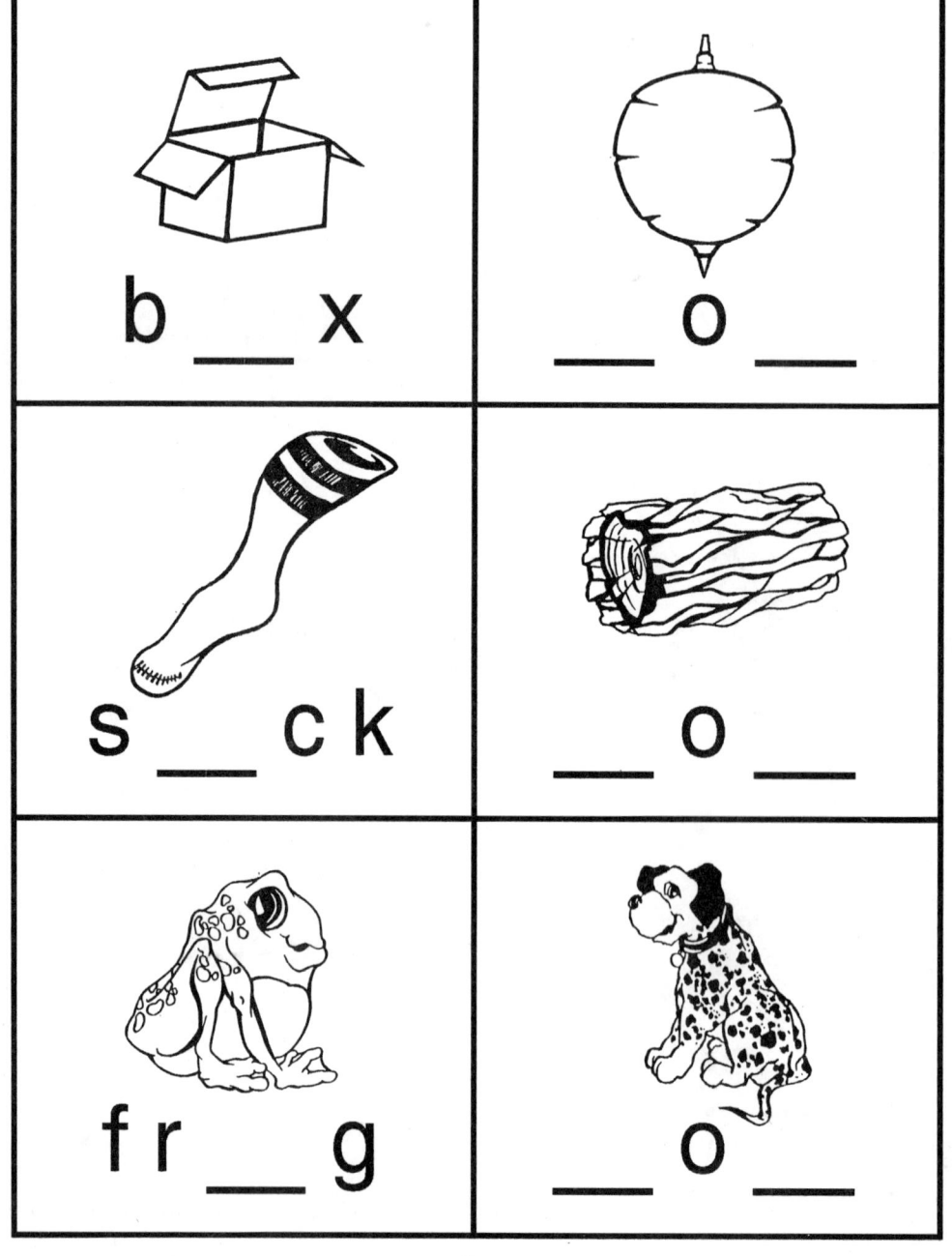

b _ x

_ o _

s _ c k

_ o _

f r _ g

_ o _

Short Vowel "u"

Short "u" sounds like the "u" in sun.

Add the correct letters to the words below. Say each word.

d _ c k

_ u _

_ u _

_ u _

_ u _

d r _ m

Short Vowel Review

Circle the short vowel that has the same sound as the picture.

fan **i** a	box **o** u	fish a **i**
pig e **i**	net a **e**	bed u **e**
bib **i** u	sun e **u**	hand **a** i
cup **u** a	duck **u** a	sock **o** u

Long Vowels
a i o u silent e

Circle the pictures in each row that have the same long vowel sound as the first picture.

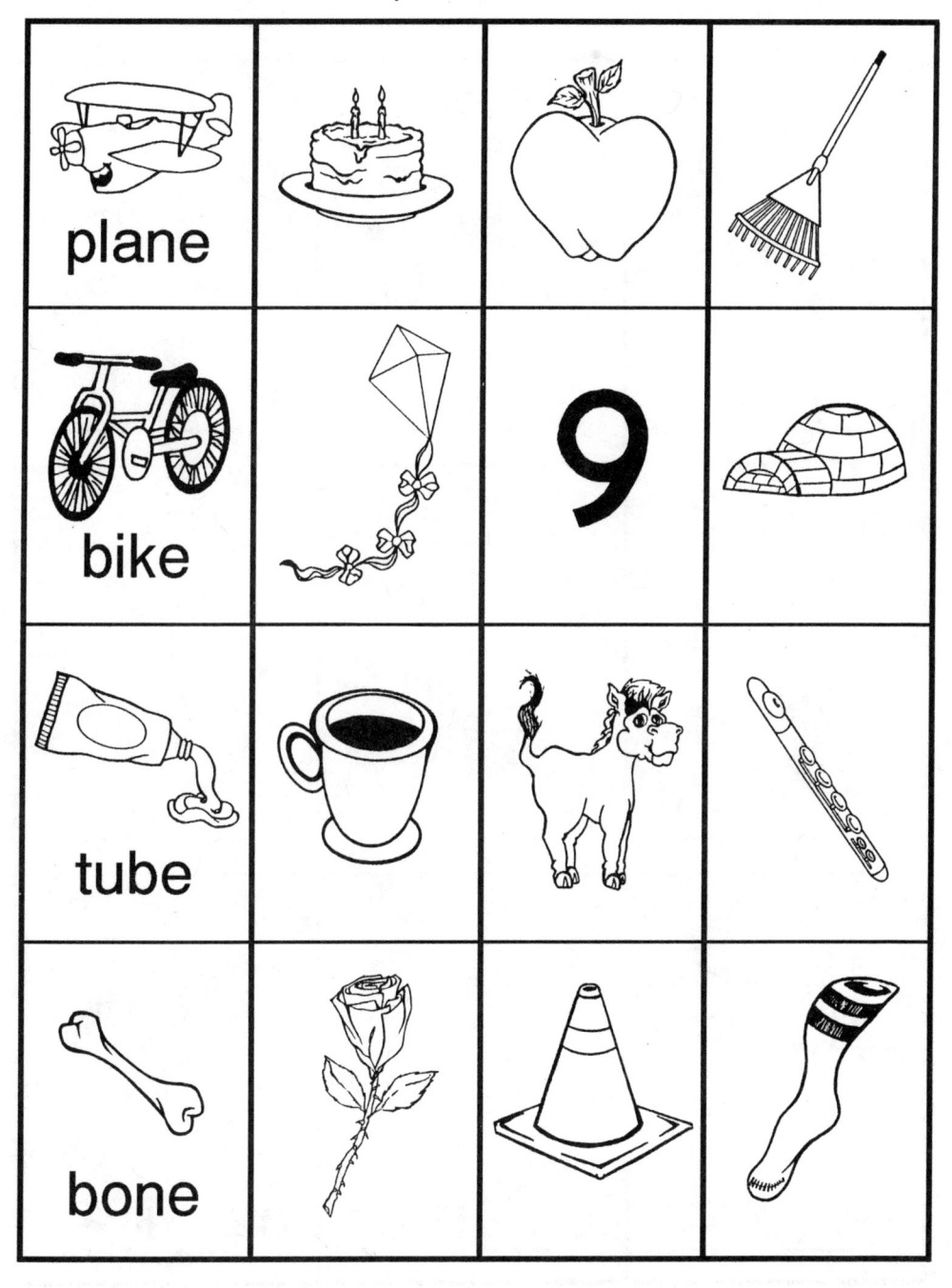

Long Vowels
a i o u silent e

Write the correct long vowel and the silent "e" in each blank.

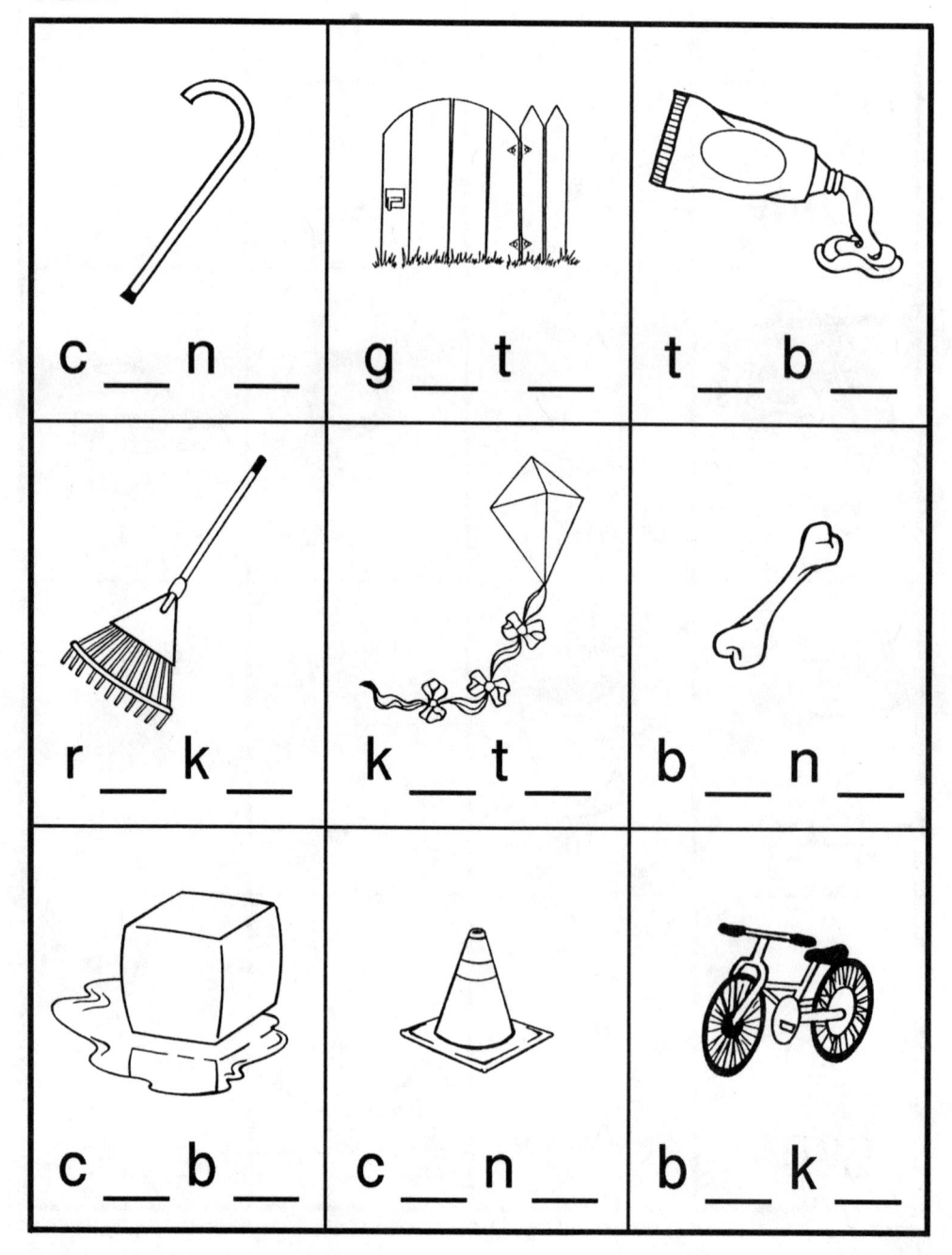

c _ n _	g _ t _	t _ b _
r _ k _	k _ t _	b _ n _
c _ b _	c _ n _	b _ k _

Long Vowels
a i o u silent e

Say each picture. Circle its correct name.

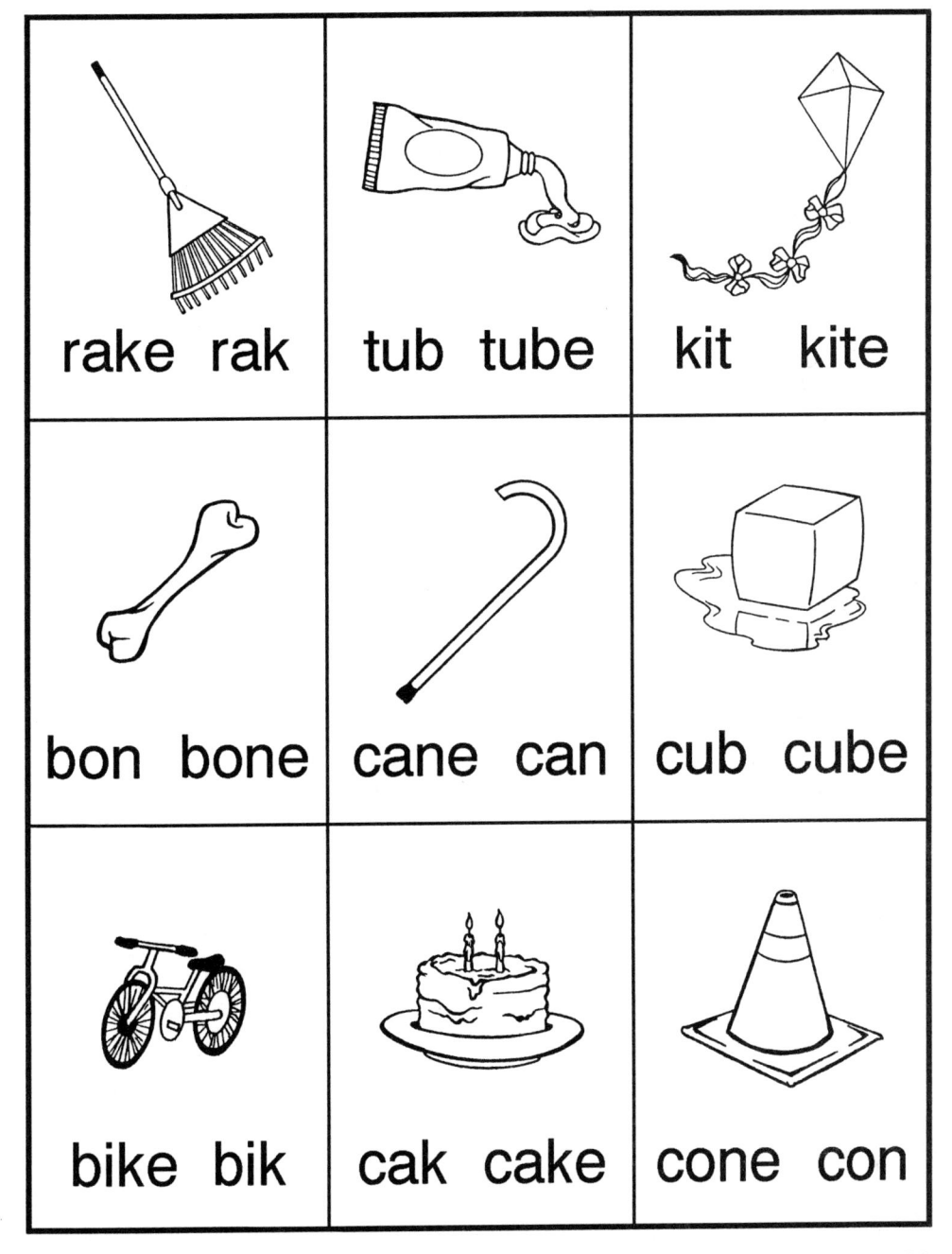

rake rak	tub tube	kit kite
bon bone	cane can	cub cube
bike bik	cak cake	cone con

Long Vowel Sounds
ai ea ee oa ue

Circle the long vowel pair that will complete each word.

s ___ p oa ee	sh ___ p ue ee	p ___ nt ai oa
l ___ f ai ea	gl ___ ue ee	c ___ t ea oa
sn ___ l ee ai	p ___ nut ea ue	qu ___ n ee ai

Long Vowel Sounds
ee oa

Circle the pictures that have the long "e" vowel sound like tree.

Put an "X" over the pictures that have the long "o" vowel sound like boat.

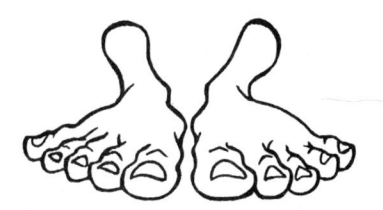

Long Vowel Sounds
ea ai

Circle the pictures that have the long "e" vowel sound like leaf.

Put an "X" over the pictures that have the long "a" vowel sound like pail.

Y As A Vowel

Color the balloon blue if the final Yy makes the long "e" sound.
Color the balloon yellow if the final Yy makes the long "i" sound.

Word Box
pony
cry
sky
bunny
puppy
lady
fly
baby
penny

Lyrics - Consonants

Once upon a time in a school quite near
a wonderful teacher did appear
She said, "It's about time you learned
 your letter sounds.
Get in your seats - Let's gather round."

Reading is important as you have learned
and letters and sounds they make up words
So - starting from the top repeat what I say
Vowels and consonants are here to stay!

Chorus:
Consonants are letters
Their sounds you will hear
Learn the letter and its sound
Learn to read this year!

B is the letter. What sound does it make?
It goes ... **bb bb**. That's great!

Say   bear
       boy
       bat
       bike

The letter B you'll learn in time
Say new words and make them rhyme.

C is the letter it has a hard sound
It goes ... **kk kk** as in cat and cake

Say   comb
       candy
       cup
       coat

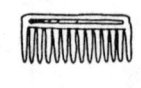

C is the letter it has a soft sound
It goes ... **ss ss** as in city and cent

Say   circus
       cymbal
       celery
       city

The two sounds of the letter C
You need to learn them both - Take it from me.

D is the letter. What sounds does it make?
It goes ... **dd dd**. That's great!

Say   dog
       dance
       duck
       dime

The letter D you'll learn in time
Say new words and make them rhyme.

F is the letter. What sound does it make?
It goes ... **ff ff**. That's great!

Say   fish
       fun
       fan
       feather

Now it's time for a little review
Listen to me and the rhythms too!

The sound of **B** is _____
The hard **C** sound is _____
The soft **C** sound is _____
The sound of **D** is _____
The sound of **F** is _____

Now's your turn for a little review
Learning your letters is up to you!

The sound of **B** is _____
The hard sound of **C** is _____
The soft sound of **C** is _____
The sound of **D** is _____
The sound of **F** is _____

Chorus
Consonants are letters
Their sound you will hear
Learn the letter and its sound
Learn to read this year!

G is the letter it has a hard sound
It goes ... **ga ga** as in guppy and game.

© 1996 Twin Sisters Productions   Twin 405 - PHONICS

Lyrics - Consonants

Say   giggle
         goat
         gum
         gorilla

G is the letter it has a soft sound
It goes ... **gg gg** as in giant and gym

Say   giant
         gentle
         giraffe
         gym

The two sounds of the letter G
You need to learn - take it from me.

H is the letter. What sound does it make?
It goes ... **hh hh**. That's great!

Say   horse
         hat
         hammer
         hog

The letter H you'll learn in time
Say new words and make them rhyme.

J is the letter. What sound does it make?
It goes ... **jj jj**. That's great!

Say   jump
         jello
         jam
         jet

The letter J you'll learn in time
Say new words and make them rhyme.

K is the letter. What sound does it make?
It goes ... **kk kk**. That's great!

Say   kite
         king
         kitten
         key

The letter K you'll learn in time
Say new words and make them rhyme.

Now it's time for a little review
Listen to me and the rhythms too!

The hard **G** sound is _____
The soft **G** sound is _____
The sound of **H** is _____
The sound of **J** is _____
The sound of **K** is _____

Now's your turn for a little review
Learning your letters is up to you!

The hard **G** sound is _____
The soft **G** sound is _____
The sound of **H** is _____
The sound of **J** is _____
The sound of **K** is _____

Chorus
Consonants are letters
Their sounds you will hear
Learn the letter and its sound
Learn to read this year!

L is the letter. What sound does it make?
It goes ... **ll ll**. That's great!

Say   leaf
         love
         lobster
         leg

The letter L you'll learn in time
Say new words and make them rhyme.

M is the letter. What sound does it make?
It goes ... **mm mm**. That's great!

Say   milk
         mom
         monkey
         mail

The letter M you'll learn in time
Say new words and make them rhyme.

N is the letter. What sounds does it make?
It goes ... **nn nn**. That's great!

Lyrics - Consonants

Say　nail
　　　note
　　　name
　　　night

The letter N you'll learn in time
Say new words and make them rhyme.

P is the letter. What sound does it make?
It goes ... **pp pp**. That's great!

Say　pencil
　　　peanut
　　　purple
　　　pink

The letter P you'll learn in time
Say new words and make them rhyme.

Now it's time for a little review
Listen to me and the rhythms too!

The sound of **L** is _____
The sound of **M** is _____
The sound of **N** is _____
The sound of **P** is _____

Now's your turn for a little review
Learning your letters is up to you!

The sound of **L** is _____
The sound of **M** is _____
The sound of **N** is _____
The sound of **P** is _____

Chorus
Consonants are letters
Their sounds you will hear
Learn the letter and its sound
Learn to read this year!

Q is the letter it is followed by a U
As in quick, quiet, quilt. That's Q!

Say　queen
　　　quarter
　　　question
　　　quiz

The letter Q you'll learn in time
Say new words and make them rhyme.

R is the letter. What sound does it make?
It goes ... **rr rr**. That's great!

Say　red
　　　rabbit
　　　run
　　　rain

The letter R you'll learn in time.
Say new words and make them rhyme.

S is the letter. What sound does it make?
It goes ... **ss ss**. That's great!

Say　sun
　　　silly
　　　salt
　　　song

The letter S you'll learn in time
Say new words and make them rhyme.

T is the letter. What sound does it make?
It goes ... **tt tt**. That's great!

Say　toad
　　　tent
　　　table
　　　turkey

The letter T you'll learn in time
Say new words and make them rhyme.

Now it's time for a little review
Listen to me and the rhythms too!

The sound of **Q** is _____
The sound of **R** is _____
The sound of **S** is _____
The sound of **T** is _____

Now's your turn for a little review
Learning your letters is up to you!

© 1996 Twin Sisters Productions　　18　　Twin 405 - PHONICS

Lyrics - Consonants

The sound of **Q** is _____
The sound of **R** is _____
The sound of **S** is _____
The sound of **T** is _____

Chorus
Consonants are letters
Their sounds you will hear
Learn the letter and its sound
Learn to read this year!

V is the letter. What sound does it make?
It goes ... **vv vv**. That's great!

Say van
     visit
     vest
     vine

The letter V you'll learn in time
Say new words and make them rhyme.

W is the letter. What sound does it make?
It goes ... **ww ww**. That's great!

Say water
     weather
     win
     worm

The letter W you'll learn in time
Say new words and make them rhyme.

X is the letter at the front you will see
It will often sound like the letter Z.

Mrs. Thompson, I know the answer to that,
It's xylophone; as a matter of fact.

X is the letter. It's unusual my friend.
For its sound is often found on the end.

Say box
     fox
     mix
     fix

The letter X you'll learn in time
Say new words and make them rhyme.

Y is the letter. What sounds does it make?
It goes ... **yy yy**. That's great!

Say yummy
     yellow
     yard
     yo-yo

Listen Y can be a vowel as in baby and cry
At the end of a word when you spy a y
You'll hear a vowel as in e or i
Turn this tape over and we'll show you why

The letter Y you'll learn in time
Say new words and make them rhyme.

Z is the letter. What sound does it make?
It goes ... **zz zz**. That's great!

Say zebra
     zipper
     zero
     zoo

The letter Z you'll learn in time
Say new words and make them rhyme.

Now it's time for a little review
Listen to me and the rhythms too!

The sound of **V** is _____
The sound of **W** is _____
The sound of **X** is _____
The sound of **Y** is _____
The sound of **Z** is _____

Now's your turn for a little review
Learning your letters is up to you!

The sound of **V** is _____
The sound of **W** is _____
The sound of **X** is _____
The sound of **Y** is _____
The sound of **Z** is _____

Chorus Ending
Consonants are letters
Their sounds you will hear
Learn the letter and its sound
Learn to read this year!

Phonics Lyrics - Vowels

Vowels are letters with different sounds
Depending on what consonant's hangin' around

We have long vowels and short ones too
We'll learn their sounds and when we're through

You'll read and write new words and more
So now it's time to explore

Listen to the sounds that short vowels make
    a   e   i   o   u

short a sounds like	aa	cat on the mat
short e sounds like	ee	hen in the pen
short i sounds like	i i	pig with a wig
short o sounds like	oo	fox in the box
short u sounds like	uu	bug on a rug

Let's learn our vowels startin' with **A**
Listen to the story - we're learnin' today

Say   1   2   123

Once upon a time a cat on a mat
grabbed a rat with a big black hat.
The rat said, "Hey, you big fat cat,
What are you doing grabbin' my hat?"

Cat and mat, rat and hat
have the short **a** sound - What about that?

Repeat the words - Let's start with **a**
The short sound you will hear. Hooray!

Say   man
       bat
       hand
       bag
       nap
       dad
       can
       ham

Listen to the sounds that short vowels make
    a   e   i   o   u

Let's learn our vowels - **E**'s the next one
Listen to the story and we'll have some fun!

Say   1   2   123

Once upon a time a hen in a pen
decided to send a letter to Ben
Ben said "Thanks, for the letter my friend
You sure are swell for a hen in a pen."

Hen and pen, Ben and friend
Have the short **e** sound like red and bed

Repeat the words, **e** is the sound
Listen to the short **e** words I've found

Say   pet
       ten
       web
       met
       bell
       men
       jet
       yes

Listen to the sounds that short vowels make
    a   e   i   o   u

Let's learn our vowels, **I**'s really neat
Listen to the music - stay with the beat.

Say   1   2   123

Once upon a time a pig with a wig
Went to a dance and did a little jig
He grinned when he saw that silly pink pig
and said "I dig that pig with a wig."

pig and wig, jig and big
have the short **i** sound - Can you dig?

Phonics Lyrics - Vowels

Repeat the words, **i** is the sound
Shout out loud - We're learnin' bound

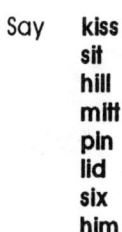

Say   **kiss**
        sit
        hill
        mitt
        pin
        lid
        six
        him

Listen to the sounds that short vowels make
    a   e   i   o   u

Let's learn our vowels the next one's **o**
Listen to the music and off we go

Say   1   2   123

Once upon a time a fox in a box
Had a friend Ox with dirty socks
The Ox said, "Hey, Mr. Fox in the box.
Please come out and wash my socks."

fox and box, ox and socks
have the short **o** sound - This song really rocks!

Repeat the words with the short sound of **o**
And soon the vowels in the words you'll know.

Say   **hot**
        mop
        rock
        pot
        top
        mom
        fox
        hop

Listen to the sounds that short vowels make
    a   e   i   o   u

Let's learn our vowels the last one's **U**
Listen to the story, 'cause we're almost through

Say   1   2   123

Once upon a time a bug on a rug
scared all the animals while acting quite smug
His friends said "That's not funny Mr. Bug
and gave that rug a great big tug.

Bug and rug, smug and tug
Have the short **u** sound, now give me a hug!

Repeat the words with the short sound of **u**
You've learned a lot and your teacher too

Say   **rug**
        bus
        nut
        run
        mud
        cup
        fun
        tub

Listen to the sounds that short vowels make
    a   e   i   o   u

Now for a story with our short vowel friends
Listen for the short vowel sounds again

The cat on mat said, "Hi Mr. Hen!
Do you like your home in a red little pen?"
"I do, I do and so does Mrs. Pig.
Have you ever met my friend with the wig?"
"No, I haven't but how do you do?"
"Pleased to meet a new friend or two."
The fox in the box said, "What about me?
I'd love a friend - two or three."
"Not I, not I," said the bug on the rug.
And that's when they all gave the bug a big hug!

Listen to the sounds that short vowels make
    a   e   i   o   u

So vowels are letters with different sounds
Depending on what consonant's hangin' around.

We have long vowels and short ones too!
But now it's time for the long vowel zoo!

Listen to the sounds that long vowels make
    a   e   i   o   u

Phonics Lyrics - Vowels

long a sounds like   aa   Ape with a cape
long e sounds like   ee   Seal made a deal
long i sounds like   i i   Mice with advice
long o sounds like   oo   Toad on a road
long u sounds like   uu   Mule with a rule

Let's learn our vowels startin' with **A**
Listen to the story - We're learnin' today

Say   1   2   123

Once upon a time an ape with a cape
Ran around the block but was out of shape
He decided to eat some chocolate cake
But later said "What a mistake!"

Ape and cape, shape and cake
Have the long a sound like take and make

Repeat the words - Let's start with **a**
The long sound you will hear ... Hooray!

Say   gate
       lake
       cane
       date
       cage
       name
       page
       game

Listen to the sounds that long vowels make
    a   e   i   o   u

Let's learn our vowels, **E**'s the next one
Listen to the story and we'll have some fun!

Say   1   2   123

Once upon a time a seal made a deal
For he was hungry for a tasty meal
He said, "I'll seek a place on the beach
Unless my meal is out of reach!"

Seal and deal, beach and reach
Have the long **e** sound - What a relief!

Repeat the words - **e** is the sound
Listen to the long **e** words I've found

Say   jeep
       feet
       leaf
       bee
       meat
       read
       week
       tea

Listen to the sounds that long vowels make
    a   e   i   o   u

Let's learn our vowels -**I**'s really neat
Listen to the music - stay with the beat

Say   1   2   123

Once upon a time I slipped on the ice
But met some mice with good advice
They said "The snow will melt and
      the sun will shine"
So get on your feet and don't you whine!"

Shine and whine, ice and mice
Have the long **i** sound - Isn't that nice?

Repeat the words, **i** is the sound
Shout out loud - We're learnin' bound

Say   kite
       hide
       five
       pipe
       bite
       ride
       fine
       size

Listen to the sounds that long vowels make
    a   e   i   o   u

Let's learn our vowels the next one is **O**
Listen to the music and off we go

Say   1   2   123

© 1996 Twin Sisters Productions   Twin 405 - PHONICS

Phonics Lyrics - Vowels

Once upon a time a toad on the road
Was very impressed when he met Miss Toad
He said, "Be my wife and you'll sit on a throne
And then you'll never have to be alone."

Toad and road, throne and alone
Have the long **o** sound like bone and cone

Repeat the words with the long sound of **o**
And soon the vowels in the words you'll know

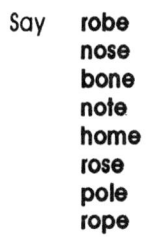

Say   robe
        nose
        bone
        note
        home
        rose
        pole
        rope

Listen to the sounds that long vowels make
   a   e   i   o   u

Let's learn our vowels the last one's **U**
Listen to the story 'cause we're almost through

Say   1   2   123

Once upon a time a mule with a rule
Said "I study hard while I'm in school.
My teacher thinks I'm really cute
Especially when I wear my new blue suit."

Mule and rule, cute and suit
Have the long **u** sound like tune and flute

Repeat the words with the long sound of **u**
You've learned a lot and your teacher too!

Say   mule
        tune
        huge
        cute
        tube
        rule
        juice
        suit

Listen to the sounds that long vowels make
   a   e   i   o   u

Now for a story with our long vowel friends
Listen for the long vowel sounds again!

The ape with a cape said "Hi Mr. Seal.
I hear you made yourself quite a deal."
"I did, I did with the help of some mice.
You know they really gave me good advice!"
"Is that so?" said the handsome toad
Who happened to hop on down the road.
"Did you hear the wonderful news Mr. Mule?"
Rhythm, Rhyme and Read is the teaching tool.

Listen to the sounds that long vowels make
   a   e   i   o   u

Before this song is done my friend
there's one more vowel when it's at the end-

Of a word when you see the letter **Y**
It'll sound like the vowels **e** or **i**

In one syllable words like buy and cry
the letter **Y** sounds like long **i**.

Say   my
        why
        try
        fly
        sky
        dry
        cry
        spy

In two syllable words like happy you'll see
The sound of **Y** is like long **e**

Say   bunny
        city
        penny
        lady
        baby
        candy
        funny
        puppy

Listen to the sounds that long vowels make
   a   e   i   o   u

© 1996 Twin Sisters Productions   Twin 405 - PHONICS

Answer Key

page 3: bat, hand, fan, lamp, cat, bag

page 4: web, bell, net, bed, nest, pen

page 5: mitt, bib, pin, fish, six, gift

page 6: box, top, sock, log, frog, dog

page 7: duck, bus, jug, cup, bug, drum

page 8: a, o, i, i, e, e, i, u, a, u, u, o

page 9: cake rake, kite nine, mule flute, hose, cone

page 10: cane, gate, tube, take, kite, bone, cube, cone, bike

page 11: rake, tube, kite, bone, cane, cube, bike, cake, cone

page 12: soap, sheep, paint, leaf, glue, coat, snail, peanut, queen

page 13: "e" = feet, sheep, cheese   "o" = coat, soap, toad

page 14: "e" = peanut, read, sleep   "a" = paint, snail, train

page 15: blue balloons = pony, bunny, puppy, lady, baby, penny

yellow balloons = cry, sky, fly